THE
2009
GRIFFIN
POETRY
PRIZE
ANTHOLOGY

The 2009 Griffin Poetry Prize Anthology

A SELECTION OF THE SHORTLIST

Edited by MICHAEL REDHILL

ANANSI

This edition published in 2009 by
House of Anansi Press Inc.
110 Spadina Avenue, Suite 801
Toronto, ON, M5V 2K4
Tel. 416-363-4343
Fax 416-363-1017
www.anansi.ca

Distributed in Canada by
HarperCollins Canada Ltd.
1995 Markham Road
Scarborough, ON, M1B 5M8
Toll free tel. 1-800-387-0117

Distributed in the United States by
Publishers Group West
1700 Fourth Street
Berkeley, CA 94710
Toll free tel. 1-800-788-3123

House of Anansi Press is committed to protecting our natural environment. As part of our efforts, this book is printed on paper that contains 100% post-consumer recycled fibres, is acid-free, and is processed chlorine-free.

13 12 11 10 09   1 2 3 4 5

Library and Archives Canada Cataloguing in Publication

Cataloguing data available from Library and Archives Canada

Library of Congress Control Number: 2009920761

Cover design: Key Gordon Communications
Cover art: Silvia Safdie
Text design and layout: Ingrid Paulson

We acknowledge for their financial support of our publishing program the Canada Council for the Arts, the Ontario Arts Council, and the Government of Canada through the Book Publishing Industry Development Program (BPIDP).

Printed and bound in Canada

CONTENTS

PREFACE

Writing poetry in this day and age might seem to be an act of extreme faith (or madness), but if the experience of judging this year's Griffin Prize is anything to go by, it's a well-placed one. Saskia Hamilton, Dennis O'Driscoll, and I read almost five hundred books of poetry this late-winter, and we were struck over and over by the continuing freshness of the art form and the level of invention, commitment, and passion among its practitioners. Should we be surprised that, in this era of dumbing-down, poetry should show itself to be this vital still? Or is it one of the side-effects of our world's various logics of reduction that an art form which distils human experiences to their essences should prove to be so durable?

The Griffin Poetry Prize throws open a door on a year's worth of international poetry, and the variety of production can be overwhelming (never mind the number of boxes that come to the judges' doors). It is also reassuring, and even moving, to see what kinds of risks are being taken — invention, even wild experimentation, is well in evidence, and surprising new inroads are still being made into old forms. Young writers are finding the art form a worthy place to take risks, and established authors showed us that there is no limit to the deepenings experience provides.

But there is another side to judging prizes, as the giving of awards to works of art is a fraught business. A life in art is a difficult and courageous thing, and individuals and foundations that choose to invest in art — whether through grants or prizes — deserve beatification. This particular prize, endowed by Scott Griffin, speaks to the possibilities of philanthropy when undertaken by a genuinely engaged and enlightened citizen. And yet... no one chooses to be an artist to be named the winner of anything, and no juror takes pleasure in the impossibility of paying tribute to everything he or she loves.

Although our jury process ended in the selection of seven magnificent collections, it began with painfully turning aside book after book, almost every one of them of some merit, the product of serious and solitary application by someone who deserves to be heard. Perhaps it is not unexpected that at the end of our task, it is this host of the turned-away that my heart aches for. Anyone who writes knows, or should remind themselves, that the quiet and solitude of creation is where everything that matters occurs. And again and again, Dennis and Saskia and I were witnesses to the brilliant heat of creation; it reconfirmed for us that there is no true first place in the making of art, only the making itself.

But however sadly we shed books from the submissions, we found that the riches of what was left behind were ample reward for our work. For the Canadian shortlist, we selected Kevin Connolly's *Revolver* for its startling inventiveness and often very funny existential orchestrations; Jeramy Dodds' brilliant debut collection *Crabwise to the Hounds*, which delighted us with its quicksilver intelligence; and A. F. Moritz's *The Sentinel*, a moving, complex collection with a deep moral purpose. The four books that comprise our international shortlist are Mick Imlah's *The Lost Leader*, a book that literally reinvents Scots mythology in poems of startling newness and beauty; Derek Mahon's *Life on Earth*, which shows this renowned Irish poet at the height of his powers writing poems of incredible beauty; C. D. Wright's American epic *Rising, Falling, Hovering*, an astonishing political work that erases the boundary between the personal and the world; and Dean Young's *Primitive Mentor*, a collection of poems by turn hilarious, deadly, and heartbreaking from a poet who walks with seeming ease the thin line between absurdity and profundity. These seven books have earned their places on the 2009 Griffin Prize shortlist, and Dennis, Saskia, and I are confident that they will reward your close attention.

We began this process by seeking books that deserved to be set above the rest, but we have concluded not as judges, but as readers again. And in returning to our normal roles, a surprising reversal has taken place: we find *ourselves* hoping to be worthy of these books. For great works of art ask much of us and that is the chief source of their delight and their ability to change our lives. We hope they move you as much as they did us.

Michael Redhill, April 2009

INTERNATIONAL
FINALISTS

MICK IMLAH

The Lost Leader

Mick Imlah's masterful *The Lost Leader* is populated by voices and revenants that point to or joke with or slip in bits of the ballads, songs, and legends of Scotland that his elder Edwin Muir said, "No poet in Scotland now can take as his inspiration." Muir's observation or injunction invites Imlah to wonder who or what can guide him now. He answers with the beautifully idiosyncratic, local, learned, teeming poems in this startling collection — the work of twenty years. Fiercely unelegiac, the book keeps equal company with the dead and the living, in its combination of demotic, modern, and archaic speech, trading in stories of legend, prophesy, insult, sport, alcohol, love, and neglect. Haunted by forgotten figures, lost guides, the divided, leaderless, often feckless characters in Imlah's poems have to make their own way, now that "the fire of belonging was out." They find temporary forms of shelter, a room in a boarding house, a telephone box, a literary reputation. The poet ends his own book with the brilliant "Afterlives of the Poets," which draws on the company of Tennyson (celebrated therefore forgotten) and James Thomson (obscure and forgotten), musing on what's left to us of their lives and pages. He recovers the lost, leaving their books open for us. And, as his closes, he joins their company.

Muck

(AD)

Hey, we were only semi-literate
ourselves: we meant to head for Mull, not
where the blessed Kevin miscarried us,
a rank bad place with no words at all.

It was about the year dot — before
MacBrayne and the broken ice; before
Colum and Camelot, whose annals skate
over our failed attempt on Muck —

when the call came (I didn't hear it)
to rid ourselves of the Ulster roof-
and-cake mentality, and work abroad.
So we did go, in wash-tub coracles,

and hauled ashore for an hour or so, on a
black upturned platter of rock, stained
with sea-lichen and scummy pools
of barge flies and crab water.

No trees, then. No welcoming men
or women either. But out on a spur's end
we spotted a sham temple — being a few
upright poles fashioned from driftwood, which

when we straggled over to them, seemed,
without a text or rune to vent their purpose,
to have their say in fish. ('That's one
of our symbols,' said Kevin, slowly.)

. . .

The first was crude, like holy rood,
a shark hung where the Christ might be.
The crossbeam of the second, wavy,
White and queasy, was split three times

by dolphins' leaps and falls; while each
of the mounting horizontals of the next,
carved with a rogue's dash or abandon,
was a fish-beam: the worst given the arc

of a catfish — though closer to, we saw
how this was worked from a lower jaw,
the bass jaw of an ox. These three might seem
the project of a class of kids; except

for the cunning which had placed the group
of crosses, if we call them crosses,
in silhouette, against the setting sun,
her *lux in embro*; or the paler moon.

The fourth was set apart. It wore
the red back half of a toy tractor, fixed
to the neck of a pole; and strapped to the spine,
a thermos, meant to last the afternoon...

— the cairn beneath it had been plugged, once,
with a plastic helmet — that was bleached by now
. from orange to lime or yellow; and over the whole
was thrown a mongrel dress of fishnet and floats.

. . .

K saw a fifth, with his second sight,
and wasn't telling. Only, 'Back to the boats! —
It's no good, we brought the word of God
to those in hiding here, and they don't want it!'

(So we sounded in reply the child's note
of feigned frustration, masking the relief
our code forbids us to have felt, or
having felt, express.) Till as we sucked

our wicker boats and heels clear of their shingle,
he struck up from the front, bellowing out
Our Founder's Lesson, 'Study the Mountains' (strange
how the borrowed prose would fill him full of himself) —

'Study the mountains; then when you fancy
that you know the mountains, you can learn the stars.'
(Just then, Kevin, none of us rowing could
see past the grimed horizon of your neck;

and as the squall got up, you couldn't hear
half that we aimed in reply; until with the double
beating of salt and rain on our hands and face
we sank back in the bee-shape; kept at the oars.

But we will expect something to sustain us,
soon, beyond the Plough and the Sperrins.
In the meantime, here's to the gay goddess
Astarté — mother of false starts!)

The Ayrshire Orpheus

And down he went, sounding the deepest floors
Where Pluto ruled with serious Proserpine,
Still piping, till he reached their double doors
And knocked. And so he saw her, horribly thin:
Eurydice, her face all eaten in,
Curled at the feet of that disdainful pair
Who feigned surprise to see a Scotsman there.

Then Orpheus, soft and urgent, half in dread
Of what she had become: 'My bonny lass —
Hey — love — though it's better than being dead —
What's happened to your lovely lips and face?
How have they disappeared, or come to this?'
And she: 'Shoosh, pet, right now I dare not say —
But you shall hear the whole another day',

As Pluto intervened: 'Your silly wife
Has marred her face, and turned her belly barren,
Through dwelling on the home she may not have;
Mindful of Ballantrae and the view of Arran,
She finds the mills of Hell friendless and foreign;
If one could spring her now to the Ayrshire coast,
No doubt her looks would heal to their uttermost!'

So Orpheus sat before that mocking twosome
And let them have it, with his matchless voice,
Pitching 'Ye Banks and Braes' at the royal bosom;
A charming 'Ae Fond Kiss', and 'Ca' the Yowes',
And then 'My love is like a red, red rose';
Till Pluto swooned, and prickly Proserpine
Lay down her softening form upon the green.

The infernal lakes had filled with lily water,
Such was the gentle power of that recital,
When Pluto cleared his throat: 'I thank the Scot
Who wrote these songs, and you, who made them vital;
Name your own prize, and that shall be requital.'
And Orpheus begged, 'Then let me take my love
Back to that place we owned in the world above.'

Which tickled Pluto. — 'You're a bold one, Mac!
— Yet I'm inclined to grant such a request,
On this condition: should you once *look back*,
Your wife reverts to Hell of the heaviest!'
Then Orpheus clasped her freshening to his chest,
And up they strove, spiralling in their fate,
Till they had almost reached the outward gate.

If you have loved, imagine the sweet chat
The two then had, rejoining their own kind —
So can you blame him, in the midst of that,
If he should suffer a local lapse of mind?
I hate to say — she fell a yard behind —
Backward he blinked — chains belted from the deeps
And yanked Eurydice to Hell for keeps.

Poor Orpheus! He felt like some old town
Of Carrick in decline: Maybole, or Girvan,
The pubs shut down, the kids, taunting 'the clown
Who couldna face the front', on drugs from Irvine;
While dismal in the twilight of surviving
Alone with his shopping, sore to be rid of her,
He walks the roads of home a widower.

Drink v. Drugs

I was worked up about some other matter
when I saw that phone box off the Talbot Road
being smashed outwards by someone inside it,
after closing on Sunday (Sunday's the day
they all go mad on crack); which is why
I didn't as usual walk by on the other side
but advanced with a purpose, and as he swivelled
nonchalant out of the frost, grabbed his lapels,
and setting him roughly against the railings,
'What is it with you,' I asked him, 'drugs?' —

which I knew very well from his vacant expression;
and after he'd cautioned me weakly
against tearing his coat, the stoned boy
answered, matter-of-factly, 'Yes' —
and told me which ones, in a Liverpool accent.
It was here I think I said something stupid
about rugby v. football, which he ignored,
rallying rather to call me a prick
and a Good Citizen, and I thought, never mind,
I'm still going to call the police.

But that would have meant myself going into
the vandalised box, and releasing my hold,
which maybe he saw, with his pert 'Go on then';
then, something better came into his head,
that *he* would phone, since he hadn't done nothing;
and moments later he was giving the station
the lowdown on the guy in a light blue shirt
and black jeans who'd assaulted him, seeming
the worse for drink, and accused me of smashing
the phone box from which he was calling now.

When in fact I'd begun to warm to the lad —
who'd flattered my stab at authority, kept
a lid on the thing; also I couldn't be sure,
could I, that he hadn't been simply clearing away
glass that was broken already, with strong
but not violent blows of the phone.
In any case, when he started to amble off,
I did nothing to stop him; and when the blue
light came quietly round the corner I was standing
alone with nothing to say for myself but my name.

Iona

Where are you taking us, sir?
the crew needed to know;
but since by the final day
    my guiding star,
instinct and purpose both, had strayed so far
off the monitor — I found I couldn't stay
    for fear of the answer.

    To tell the truth
I had given up on youth; would only stew
in the chemical toilet, the door half-
open, a 'cry for help', till out of the blue
    a nurse ducked
from the cockpit holding you, and I
was face to face with my pilot!

. . .

In the weeks before you were born
    the head did warn
me not to give over the stage at once
to baby talk: and so we stood our ground
when from among your breathings-out were told
    two voluntary sounds,
a rudimentary yes and no.

But now, when all the words
we care about are yours, I have to tender
    our deep surrender;
as in a suit of dungarees you go
    groping your way to sense
like Milton, blind before he felt
    the wall's resistance.

. . .

Already you discern what the artist meant
in an old poster of mine, the 'Mars'
of Velazquez: the war god in his afterprime
    released too soon
from that perpetual service; sat
in his demob nakedness and gloom,
only his helmet on, almost
a souvenir, muscles smoking away,
    until you up and say
— *Poor tin soldier man!*
He's thinking about things!

. . .

My right hand is Nessie's head,
her neck my dripping arm. *How old*
is the dinosaur? Forty
    or fifty million years.
Can the dinosaur sing? No,
too old; but likes to be soothed
    by others singing.

I open her thumb-
  and-finger beak
at least to let her speak
in her quavery Triassic,
'Take me to your leader!'
— to which you instantly,
  I haven't got any leader.

. . .

What, meanwhile, are my own terms?
Darling—'little'— *Mädchen* — the same
Suspicious argot I used to spy on.

. . .

Strange, that we dwell so much
sometimes, on self and such,
that we can spend an age without
  a clear view out:
when, if I asked the mirror once
in the way of an old queen,
to frame how things might look
twenty or thirty visits thence,
all it reflected back was white
and unrefracted light, the mean
prophetics of a closed book.

Of course, it was not allowed to show
    or we to know
that you were coming all the time,
    my perfect rhyme;
how you would seize the reins, Iona,
riding my shoulders over the hill
    or rarely sitting still,
your hands spread on my knees, my jeans
    the sidelines of your throne.
Succession is easy: first it was them,
then me for a bit; and now it's you.

. . .

Granted your repertoire
    has lumps in it,
of Shrek and Cinderella;
but there's prodigious poetry too,
    a magic spring
in the sweet Cordelia thing
you once undid me with —

Let's laugh through all the days, till the water
    comes over our eyes . . .
or, which is more my line — not
mawkish, I think, or maudlin:
In Oxford Church, there are two Marys;
    one of them has got a baby
and one of them hasn't got a baby.

DEREK MAHON

Life on Earth

Formal grace, uncluttered diction, and sprightliness of
movement lend Derek Mahon's new poems a musicality
and memorability which is intensified by their visionary
gaze and their poignant yearning for unspoiled and
unsoiled places: "blue skies, / clear water, scattered light."
His light-filled work celebrates the sun's life-sustaining
powers; yet he also fears the heat of the sun in the
context of global warming: "Sea levels rising annually, /
glaciers sliding fast, / species extinct. ..." Mahon is drawn
to the lives, worlds, and work of other artists; a vivid
bio-poem, retracing Coleridge's life, and an atmospheric
poem evoking the post-war Belfast of the novelist Brian
Moore are set alongside elegant versions of Ovid (the
desolate "Ariadne on Naxos") and Ibsen (the haunting
and unsettling "The Lady from the Sea"). Visual art
features prominently too: a sequence of "Art Notes"
re-creates the paintings of Edward Hopper, Howard
Hodgkin, René Magritte, and others with meticulously
crafted mastery. An outstanding collection from one of
Ireland's most acclaimed poets.

Insomnia

Scratch of a match
fierce in the dark. The alarm clock,
night-vigilant, reads twenty minutes to four;
wide awake, as so often at this dead hour,
I gaze down at the lighted dock,
trawler and crated catch,
as if on watch.

The bright insects
of helicopters drop to the decks
of gas rigs ten miles out in the heavy waves,
their roaring rotors far from our quiet leaves,
before midnight, and the ship that shone
at dusk on the horizon
has long since gone.

Nothing stirs
in garden or silent house,
no night owl flies or none that we can hear;
not even the mild, traditional field-mouse
runs nibbling, as you'd expect, under the stairs.
Boats knock and click at the pier,
shrimps worship the stars.

The whole coast
is soporific as if lost
to echoes of a distant past —
the empty beach house with no obvious owner,
the old hotel like a wrecked ocean liner
washed up one stormy night
and left to rot.

That woman from
the Seaview, a 'blow-in'
of some kind from a foreign shore,
seems out of her element and far from home,
the once perhaps humorous eyes grown vague out here.
What is she? A Lithuanian, or a Finn?
We've met before

beside some flat
road bridge or bleak strand road,
two men in black at the corner staring hard,
far off in the stricken distance perhaps a shipyard,
chimneys, power plants, gasometers,
oil refineries, Gothic spires
and things like that —

where a cloud climbs
and swirls, yellow and red
streaking the estuary, and a soul screams
for sunken origins, for the obscure sea bed
and glowing depths, the alternative mud haven
we left behind. Once more we live in
interesting times.

The Lady from the Sea

(after Ibsen)

She Born in a lighthouse, I still find it hard
as wife to a doctor ten miles from the coast.
My home is a pleasant one but I get bored;
the mountains bother me. Now, like a ghost,
you show up here, severe and adamant.
What are you anyhow? What do you want?

He I am a simple man upon the land,
I am a seal upon the open sea.
Your eyes are of the depths. Give me your hand,
give me your heart and come away with me
to the Spice Islands, the South Seas; anywhere.
Only the force of habit keeps you here.

She Even up here, enclosed, I sniff the brine,
the open sea out there beyond the beach;
my thoughts are waves, my dreams are estuarine
and deeper than an anchor chain could reach.
I knew you'd come, like some demonic fate
glimpsed at a window or a garden gate.

He How can you live here with no real horizon,
someone like you, a mermaid and a Muse,
a figment of your own imagination,
the years elapsing like a tedious cruise?
Your settled life is like this summer glow;
dark clouds foreshadow the approaching snow.

She Sometimes, emerging from my daily swim
or gazing from the dock these quiet nights,
I know my siren soul; and in a dream
I stare astonished at the harbour lights,
hugging my knees and sitting up alone
as ships glide darkly past with a low moan.

He If our mad race had never left the sea,
had we remained content with mud and rock,
we might have saved ourselves great misery;
though even this evening we might still go back.
Think of the crashing breakers, the dim haze
of a salt sun rising on watery days.

She My wild spirit unbroken, should I return
to the tide, choosing at last my other life,
reverting to blue water and sea-brine,
or do I continue as a faithful wife?
If faithful is the word for one who clings
to the lost pre-existence of previous things.

He Do you remember the great vow you made
to the one man you chose from other men?
The years have come between, with nothing said,
and now the stranger has appeared again
to claim your former love and make it new.
You ask me what I am; but what are you?

She I am a troubled woman on the land,
I am a seal upon the open sea,
but it's too late to give my heart and hand
to someone who remains a mystery.
Siren or not, this is my proper place;
go to your ship and leave me here in peace.

Art Notes

1 A LIGHTHOUSE IN MAINE

— *Edward Hopper*

It might be anywhere, that ivory tower
reached by a country road. Granite and sky,
it faces every which way with an air
of squat omniscience, intensely mild,
a polished Buddha figure warm and dry
beyond vegetation; and the sunny glare
striking its shingled houses is no more
celestial than the hot haze of the world.

Built to shed light but also hoarding light,
it sits there dozing in the afternoon
above the ocean like a ghostly moon
patiently waiting to illuminate.
You make a left beyond the town, a right,
you turn a corner and there, ivory-white,
it shines in modest glory above a bay.
Out you get and walk the rest of the way.

2 THE REALM OF LIGHT

— René Magritte

The picture in the picture window shows
a poplar, is it, a house calm and clear
at dawn or dusk, a lamp post's yellow light
abuzz on shutters and a shivering pond.
Poplar and roof aspire though, point beyond
the upstairs reading lamp to another sphere
where, behind deckled leaves, pacific rows
of cloud file slowly past, serenely white.

It must be dusk, with the light almost gone,
but view this picture with extreme distrust
since what you see is the *trompe-l'oeil* of dream.
It *might* be dusk, with the house almost dead;
or is there somebody getting out of bed,
the exhausted street light anxious for a rest,
birds waking in the trees, the clouds astream
in an invisible breeze? It must be dawn.

— Maurice Wilks

North light on the snowlight on a little bridge
where once we loitered during a previous age
in the quiet dusk of one more summer day
as the sun went down behind the Antrim hills
and Scotland dimly shone across the water.
Girls watched the boys go by, the boys the girls,
the Lavery sisters and the postman's daughter;
later we'd flirt with them at Lynn's Café.

Wilks never bothered with 'the picture plane',
with 'colour values' and the fancy words —
as for aesthetics, that was for the birds.
They slept in a yellow trailer at Shane's Cairn
where, every morning, he would paint the world:
hedges, fields, the sunlight on the river,
the forest and the dunes, a still unspoiled
paradise we thought would last for ever.

Homage to Gaia

1 ITS RADIANT ENERGIES

A world of dikes and bikes
    where yoghurt-weavers drive
on gin and margarine...
    This is how to live

in the post-petroleum age,
    gathering light-beams
to run the house with clean
    photoelectric frames

that trap the sun and focus
    its radiant energies;
their glow reflects the seasons,
    cloud cover, open skies.

Our micro-climate gives us
    gentle winters here.
Spring starts in January
    and lasts throughout the year

with its perennial flowers,
    so even an average annual
thousand kilowatt hours
    per photovoltaic panel

looks feasible in time.
    What you notice about
the panes is their composure,
    their heliotropic quiet

as star-gazing, rain-laced,
    light-drinking polysilicon
raises its many faces
    to worship the hot sun.

Great sun, dim or bright,
    eye in the changing sky,
send us warmth and light!
    We can never die

while you are roaring there
    in serial rebirth
far from our atmosphere.
    Remember life on Earth!

A cold and stormy morning.
    I sit in Ursula's place
and fancy something spicy
    served with the usual grace

by one of her bright workforce
    who know us from before,
a nice girl from Tbilisi,
    Penang or Baltimore.

Some red basil linguine
    would surely hit the spot,
something light and shiny,
    mint-yoghurty and hot;

a frosty but delightful
    pistachio ice-cream
and some strong herbal
    infusion wreathed in steam.

Once a tomato sandwich
    and a pint of stout would do
but them days are over.
    I want to have a go

at some amusing fusion
    Thai and Italian both,
a dish of squid and pine-nuts
    simmered in lemon broth,

and catch the atmospherics,
    the happy lunchtime crowd,
as the cold hand gets warmer
    and conversation loud.

Boats strain at sea, alas,
    gales rattle the slates
while inside at Ursula's
    we bow to our warm plates.

Homage to Goa

The ceiling fans in the house go round and round
as if to whisk us off to a different sky.
I squirt Deet at a thin mosquito whine;
gods chuckle softly from a garden shrine,
fruit ripen in the gloaming without a sound.
Shiva, Parvati and Ganesh the elephant boy
promote the comical to the sublime; though, shown
a choice of deities, I defer like most
to violet Krishna in the heat and dust,
brother of Dionysus, expert in everything —
flute-player, hero and lecher, comedian, king.

I rock on a warm veranda as daylight goes.
The hippies too revered him in the old days
of hair and beads, torchlight and techno trance,
trailing from poppy field to lamasery
as irksome and imperious as Camões.
It's snowing in Kashmir, but here in Goa
we already have spring temperatures. Anandu
waters the earth and brushes up the sand.
Banana leaves and plantains in a daze
trade oxygen for tar; *tat tvam asi.*
Already a heavy mango strikes the ground.

A mozzie once myself, *I* buzzed and bit —
but only foot and elbow, ear and knee;
a cheeky monkey keen on human thought,
with a reach greater than my grasp, I'd dance
wildly at times, conscious of ignorance,

or chew on my own morose inadequacy.
Still, I behaved, and so the next time out
I got to sit to a half-mad sadhu
at Brahmin school. 'The body is a shadow,'
said he, 'it tells you in the Upanishads';
but spirit knows no slapstick or romance.

Clouds dream the people and we spread like plants,
waves smash on beaches for no obvious purpose
except to deliver the down-to-earth palingenesis
of multitudinous life particles. A porpoise
revolves on the sky as if in outer space
where we started out so many aeons ago.
Goa fact file: infant mortality low,
average life expectancy seventy-five,
functional literacy sixty-nine percent;
the porcupine and flying fox survive,
also the sloth bear and shy Chital doe.

'The streaming meteor, is it dead or alive,
a deliberate thing or merely gas and stone?
Some believe in a life after this one
while others say we're only nut and leaf.
An ageing man repents his wicked ways:
we began so innocently, and may again'
— Abu al-Ma'ari, tenth century, Syrian.
Given a choice between paradise and this life
I'd choose this life with its calamities,
the shining sari, the collapsing wave,
the jeep asleep beneath the coconut trees;

skyflower, flame-of-the-forest among the palms,
ripe mangoes dropping from the many limbs,
the radio twang of a high-pitched sitar,
'Kareena Kapoor in Hot New Avatar'!
A gecko snaps a spider from a window.
Given a choice of worlds, here or beyond,
I'd pick this one not once but many times
whether as mozzie, monkey or pure mind.
The road to enlightenment runs past the house
with its auto-rickshaws and its dreamy cows
but the fans, like the galaxies, go round and round.

C. D. WRIGHT

Rising, Falling, Hovering

C. D. Wright's thirteenth collection, *Rising, Falling, Hovering*, reminds us what poetry is for. This is poetry as white phosphorus, written with merciless love and depthless anger, but it is "not a chemical weapon, it's an incendiary...it is for illumination." *Rising, Falling, Hovering* is about conflict, local and global, and how failures of the heart bring disaster on every scale. In the long poem that anchors this book, Wright ties together the war in Iraq, the war on the poor, the challenges borders present, and family crises to create a portrait of the human soul riven by separateness. It is, primarily, a red-hot political epic, in which Wright states, "to be ashamed is to be American" and that "happiness is for amateurs." And yet, how can we react to a poetry this alive with invention and purpose but with joy? In *Rising, Falling, Hovering*, C. D. Wright wakes the reader — from dreams of both a perfect world and one drowned in horror — to the saving beauty of clear sight. Over a long career marked by deep moral engagement and constant reinvention, Wright has placed herself and her readers *"at a crossroads,"* as she writes, which is not just a place, but "the very instant you stopped looking for meaning and began rifling among the folds of feeling instead where things were to be made new again...."

from Rising, Falling, Hovering

In front of a donut shop   someone's son is shot dead

A witness on condition of anonymity

The slow open vulgar mouth   drawing on a cigarette

In a face once called Forever Young

Now to be known as Never-a-Man

Gone to the world of the working and the prevaricating

of the warring   world of drywalling of lousy test scores

of fishing from a bridge on a brilliant afternoon

                    belt buckle blown undone

Recollect reading to her boy

reading to him in bed   overcome herself

with sleep as if drugged or slugged   then jabbed up again

Come on   Keep reading   Don't stop   Don't ever stop

like she was saying   Beauty cannot   she cannot marry

the Beast   and tonight as on all other rose-scented evens

He stumbles   the Beast he stumbles   from Beauty's empty chamber

In agony   he goes in agony   the fur of his fingers

smoking   until it's her boy he is the one saying

exclaiming   Yes Yes he will he will marry the Beast

                until he is the one who conks out

as a light pole struck by a drunken car

And suddenly it's raining like plastic

When she stumbles at last from the room

he is the one   who shakes himself awake

and yells   Protect me   and she is the one

who promises exclaiming   Yes Yes she will   I swear

if it kills me I will   as once the mother

of Forever Young shot in front of the donut shop

must have sworn   if it killed her she will   a boy

       So quiet   the reporter heard from his kin

You wouldn't even notice him on your electric bill

       Over there   it's a different world

       Desperate to be rejoined to this one

It is still raining like plastic

the brazen daytime rave of cicadae   cut off

In a fast fade to black   a low intensity shattering within

       to dramatize the break

Her confidential informant   is her imagination

Requests for him not to be photographed

in this position   not the flash of flesh

the powder burns that pepper the chest

You won't believe what I was dreaming

to the flash of flesh, the scarred back

                  (Do not think him healed)

Go back to sleep

It never happened

                There was a cenote

and steps dug out of the centuries

                and dogs always dogs

The hot iron on her chest she feels it now

It is her familiar   the fear   the sear

She is driving or is she   being driven

Trees and fences   fall behind   an oil truck

changes lanes   (without warning)

                The water on her right looks dead

        bird sanctuary   void of birdsong

She forgets where she is headed   a meeting

No   an errand   an appointment   is her life

comic or tragic   that card stays

facedown   she doesn't even know what hand

she's playing   or whose house belongs

to the white rhododendron

Across the river   is a whole other world:

Hotel (once grand) with a ballroom called Starlight

A lobby that smells like assisted-living dinner

smoke-discolored chandelier

Aloe vera and bromeliad felted with dust

And toenails of the truly old painted
for twirling across polished floors

And one of the old ones in a camphoric gown
says she wore this when she was smaller

Spotlights on the fountain tinted for travelers
in the time of terror   color of the koi

Wasted figure in a tall mirror

clad in ratty rags   forewarns

These are the last hours of empire or some such

inauspicious whispering   So?   What?   ¿So can I have a cigarette?

(in the absence of any foreseeable remedy)

She ran off with a fallen aristocrat an adventurer
        cut down on his burro by bandidos

Belt blown undone   wrecked down there

When she came back to US
        they sent her son to Baghdad

whom she vowed to protect   if it kills her she will

There's not a troy ounce of compassion in this scenario

There is the inhuman dimension

The bridges breaking off in chunks
        of grey   libraries folding

School buildings indistinguishable from penitentiaries

Like I said to the doorman the other night

Some moon, huh

You should have seen it before the war Miss

We must not get used to this

                                            to be cont.

The burros are not young   the macho a balker

The trail frays every which way

Coffee comes from bark

Tortillas made at dawn with a base of dust

Niguas bore into the soles

The brindle dog deserts

      Fleas

Cloth on the ceiling to catch scorpions

A mattress is unheard of

When there's no rawhide

A catre stretched with saplings

      Flies

A hot wind beats us off course

Warm beer or warm soda for supper

Ascent without end

Rumor of tigres and leones

These maps are worthless

      No supper

Fire moving this way

No corn for the burros

Cactus for privacy

Ticks

Pigs are another bother

No breakfast

The landmark mahogany struck down

The brindle returns

Running low on paregoric

Snake

Cactus for shade

Running low on water

Smoking husks

The macho with an ulcerated back

One of us with dysentery y yo embarazada

A woman con pistola y cuchillo

Wears his trousers for comfort

Riding low

A boy the señora says

Fifty pesos

Hands washed with mescal

He will pass out

In the corn crib

He will cut the cord he will

Cut it with his teeth

It devolved on her to speak through the shadows of events themselves:

Animals or men passing through the night
al otro lado

Without documents, blankets, contacts,
without water, without *with*

Freeze, dehydrate, burn

A knot of unmoving human forms
waiting for a bell to quicken them

from pueblo without medicine maize or milk

from colonia of cardboard without fuel or flour

Mira: you will never see faces like this again

These are the ones who loved you   these the ones who hurt

Chihuahuan sun sizzles in its blackened trim

Now moving at the speed of laudanum.

Treading sand and dust under the big dry socket of god

Discarding the shawl   the straw hat that protected nada

Desert floor entering memory hole

Ants beginning their business from the inside

The drag road unavoidable

Every footfall a giveaway unless

One could vault out of the broken saddle
al otro lado   Farm Road 170

Without disturbing the particulate surface of earth
the way ghosts go back and forth

so that the famous black carriage of Juárez was also told to pass

Under the cover of tarbush
copperhead of their anonymity

Juan e Juana Doe
One last exhalation of earthly hell   breath chopped in half by a border

One last fata morgana   unless the reflection is not water but light

Unless the lights are the migra

Unless one does not know one could not in fact see to see

Unless one does not know that what one is hearing
is the simmer of one's very stomach in one's very blood   sopa de pollo

Dark meat breaking off in chunks

The last pinch of salt spent with the last wick of sweat

Unless one does not know that what one is hearing
is the crashing of one's skeleton   chandelierlike

Like they say in Iraq   Now fear up harsh

DEAN YOUNG

Primitive Mentor

Dean Young is a high-energy poet of copious invention and bold imagination. His vigorous, vibrant, fast-paced poems make startling connections between highly improbable things as they take the measure of a world too variegated and complex to be fully comprehended, a "world so full/of detail yet so vague." A Dean Young poem may set off from anywhere ("I am not a flower. / I am a chunk of meat/sprayed by the department store cosmetic technicians") and may lead anywhere ("My real mother burst into flame/smoking a Chesterfield in a paper shift"). His zany wit and hyperactive surrealism are all the more compelling for their capacity to suddenly morph into an elegiac register, marked by piquant ruminations on evanescence, mortality, and death. As entertaining as they are original, as resourceful as they are beguiling, Young's mesmeric poems convey a uniquely accurate sense of life as it is experienced in the fraught and tumultuous circumstances of the globalized twenty-first century.

Self Search

When we look around for proof
of basic epistemological matters,
that life isn't only seemings smattered,
a dream brought on by snaggled meat,
often the self blocks the view
of the tree or cat or car race
so all we find are me-leaves, me-meows,
me-machines of speedy impulse-me.
Maybe the point's to see the self
as a kind of film that tints everything
bluer, more you-er and yet look through,
whatever you have to do, volunteer
at a shelter changing the abandoned
hamster's litter, put together a coat drive
for the poor, go door to door for your candidate,
be devoted to a lover or lose yourself
cheering in a crowd, Go Hens! Go
higher, go lower, to see perhaps the sky
as a rock might, meditate until you become
a beam of light, be divided as a 3 by 27
and not get overcome by your identity ending
or expect to reappear after the decimal.
Perhaps you should be practicing not having
a self to claim, one day it's baggage
we're without, no longer waiting
for it to squirt out onto the conveyor belt
with all the others that look so much alike.
Yet it is sad to imagine no me around
to press his nose into your sleeping hair.

I worry death won't care, just a bunch of dust
rushing up, some addled flashes, chills
then nil. I like too much that old idea
of heaven, everyone and pet you've lost
runs up which could not happen
if there's no me there to greet.
Self, I'm stuck with you
but the notion of becoming unglued is too much
and brings tears that come, of course,
because you're such a schmuck. Some days
you crash about raving how ignored you are
then why the hell don't people let you alone
but I've seen you too perform small
nobilities, selfless generosities.
One way or the other, we'll part I'm sure
and you'll take me with you?

Gruss

Whenever I'm not drunk enough
is a waste of time.
I carry within me a hypnagogic dawn,
maybe the insulation gnawed by rats,
maybe I'll never be back.
Ha ha to the mating swans.
Ha ha to the sepulchral golden slime
that shines and shines and shines.
This party started long before I arrived
with the last of wacko youthful chatter,
a curious crew, prone to slam-dance depression.
What's the matter? Don't know, maybe so
much hilarity is a strain on us or at least
we like to boast in loopy communiqués
to those who've seen through us
and love us for what they see,
maybe some trees, a packing factory,
some secretive birdie hopping about
with a grasshopper in its mouth.
I don't know what I'd do without you
although that's how I spend most of my time.
It'd be unbearable otherwise,
like a vacation without sleeping pills,
without some creaking rain
abating the granite's breakdown.
Such a paltry gesture, my surrender.

Briar

After the final battle of the gods,
the rain tasted like iron forever.
And after forever, the worst was over
until another worst volunteered.
Not to say green tips didn't thrust
from mordent roots or nests
percolate with starlings.
Even the cockroach sports
vertiginous wings.
Pilgrim, what the fuck...?
No one knows if the chunk of ice
in the center of the chest
was part of a planet of ice
before we began
so full of impurities,
it could be flint,
it could be a soul,
each of us chipped off.
Three or four lifetimes later,
I hope I'm not the same drunkard
although the enemies are the same,
galloping against each other
over the boneyards of horses,
blowing the pump houses,
torching the bell towers.
Three children beating
an already injured snake
make a civilization.
Agony is an art like any other

and deserves to be forgotten.
Imagination is the vacation
of meaning, thinks the snake,
the earth's other minions
come to dispose of the remains,
spine to summer hearth,
spine to winter castle.
Then the businessmen arrive
messaging the invisible
so some of us flee with our white wine.
You don't want to be around me now.
What isn't born twisted?
Even the lily leaf, the hummingbird.
There was a man who couldn't
straighten and he fell from nowhere.
Ask him and he'll say he was elected
into the new order, new orchard
where fruit can't rot or ripen.
For a sum, a mechanism
produces your future.
Can the mind function without
its scorpion? Scorpion warmed
in a corner, allowed its repose.
The ocean rubs its belly,
come sleep with me,
the surface hugely scratched,
jagged like illustrations of electricity,
thinks the woman on the porch
who in three days must move her mother
into a bottle of antiseptic
because she's leaving the oven on.
Obscene abbreviations.

When the man comes out, clinking
his ice, she has already turned
into six or seven other people,
each with a necklace of tiny skulls,
a strange power, a debt.
The snake was already dead
by anyone's account.
It was a small thing getting smaller.
It was the animal you were
before the animal you've become.
A boy has found a bullet
by the swing-set.
Something's written on it.

Fire Ode

What gift is this the day forces
upon the hapless tangerine tree?
It is the gift of sunlight for chlorophyll
to do what it will in the continuing
nourishment of the tree and me
who its fruit is chewed by, swallowed
mixed with digestive juices and ransacked
for fuel just as the fire ransacks air
for oxygen to bind gasses to, what
it frees from the thoughtless-looking
wood. Behind, it leaves a heap
of smudgy stuff lesser than a dream
that can not be recalled. Of what
was once a house, a lawn or limb
or nearly anything fire fancies.
Oh, what fun to quaff the ignited
tequila shot and la la feel hot
flame-o all things revealed
burning with their secret being
like a frog-pond with frogs, obviously
the pianist, not so much the cinder block
but it too runs a temperature, fever of itself.
So praise the flicker and the power
even though it abbreviates us ash.
Better to dash than never go at all,
the error is not to fall but to fall
from no height. Or so's the argument
of Andrew Marvell as long as his poem lasts.
Which turns out could be forever although
coy mistress and himself long cinder and dust be.

Either that or rust like a busted tractor
abandoned in a snowy field now suitable
for only artsy photographs that speak
of loneliness and passion spent
as well as peaceable, elegant resignation
which makes me want to scream.

Lives of the Primitives

Shouldn't someone have run for help by now?
When I was a child someone was always running for help.
None returned

but I still like to think of them snookered in phlox,
sucking on a hookah, getting the lowdown from the giant worm.
Everyone was wiser then, knew better,
the same force at work in the campfire
as the apocalypse, no one was excluded

except those who disqualified themselves
by being poor and dirty, not speaking proper English,
low scores, fidgeting during naptime, the deranged.
I knew I was one of them
or would be soon enough
once my sinecure gave out

and I'd crash among the pickpockets and divorcees,
dictionary readers, addicts of the instant,
kids with stigmata and spectacular tits,
intemperate artistic folk
counterfeiting wounds for a public
that could never hurt enough.
Obviously, I'm damaged goods,

even in my three-piece some kind of dictum
from the ant world eats at my nonchalance.
Sure I'd left some broken hearts behind
I don't mind saying and won't be getting
any refunds soon. A new pod of recruits
paces off the wrestling rink, Harvard is in the air.
There's so much we still don't know:

the life expectancy of a squirrel, the lair
of the giant squid, the monetary systems
of those vanished tribes. How strange
to be among westerners again, no longer
handcuffed and strapped in plastic in the driving snows
of the second higher pass, a failed performance
I admit, not like my pal who painted everything

red. Red of swallowed shout,
red of pig's snout, he had some kind of argument
and went on to make a mill and kill himself
then really rake it in. Funny to read
what they write about him now

as if the whole thing wasn't an accident,
the radio on comic opera, the sewage
singing to the sea, the sea swinging back,
as if he wasn't someone who loved a joke
especially on himself.

Exit Exam

Difficult to believe what hurts so much
when the cement truck bounces you
off a tree trunk
is not solid knocking solid
but electron cloud repulsing electron cloud
around the overall emptiness of matter,
a clash of minuscule probabilities
in the beehive of the void.
Somehow you're only scratched and bruised
but the driver's in agony,
no license no immigration paper
a picture of his wife still in Oaxaca
five kids he sends money to
so you try to assure him you're okay
look not hurt
hopping foot to foot
which only seems to him
you've got trauma to the head
or were already loco
either way problemo.
Your bicycle bent,
he lifts it tears in his eyes
which are mirrors showing everything
on fire in black water.
This is the universal language of bent bikes,
something large and tragic writ in small words
while the world burns in black water.
Nothing will repair it
is not true

but now is not the time to bring that up.
You are both golden
pepperoncinis in the vinegar of life.
So piquant, so sad.
There is a wound where you bonked against the tree
and the tree, as usual, deals with its injuries
in good humor.
A bird in its branches had just come to life,
hideously bald, eyes unopened bulging sacks,
too delicate, too helpless
yet there is a concept of the cosmos forming
in its tiny skull. It gapes and mother
regurgitates nutritious worm.
It grows a black miter and blue belly.
Nest formation, a couple false starts then presto!
It calls its mate radiant toy.
Its mate calls back radiant toy.
It gets trapped in the science building for an hour.
Still, it understands no more
than we do that voice coming toward us
in our dented sorrow, our dark dread
saying everything will be okay.
Bright opening bright opening
where does it come from?
How can we get there?
And if we do
will we be petrified or dashed to even smaller pieces,
will we be released from the wheelhouse
or come back as hyena or mouse,
as a cloud or rock
or will it be sleep's pure peace of nothingness?

CANADIAN

FINALISTS

KEVIN CONNOLLY

Revolver

What sort of warning is being sounded in a book where the table of contents is fictional? Perhaps that the signs are not to be trusted; that you are going to have to find your own way. Such is the promise of the work of Kevin Connolly, one of Canada's most profoundly engaged and rewarding poets. *Revolver,* his fourth collection, finds him deep in the territory he has made his own: the dark place where we attempt to make sense of the noise we've been making and the sounds coming from others. Through a multiplicity of voices and attacks, maskings and menacings, Connolly conducts an existential research that only pretends to be jokey, only feints at absurdity. But this is not a light-hearted poetry of effects: it's a kind of stand-up comedy done with a flame-thrower. In *Revolver,* Connolly works subtexts of suspicion, rejecting everything received and shaking the forms to get them to reveal what there is no language for, yet. "People like people who stand for things," he writes, suggesting it's a misplaced faith, to put your trust in anything you can define. It's a courageous poetic stance, to leave yourself and your reader painted into a corner. But there's a door behind you you won't find until you're pressed up against it, and in this superb collection, Connolly shoves you through that door and out into naked space.

Terre Haute

We're used to a season progressing logically,
then, heading south by car, it suddenly
makes no sense in reverse: a race from
ice to snow, gray earth and nippled trees,
pooled water and mud, then the first white blades,
seeming to expire when they're really
cutting way for flowers. Dun, flat fields
— all at once, three brilliant bantam hens
over the wire, Technicolor peril beside the
interstate, its football-sized hawks.
Quarry, copse, mobile home, whole lives
spilling like a purse over the backyard.
Swamp, acres of razed cornfields waiting for seed
— experimental hybrids — which,
now you think of it, is odd, seeing as corn
really isn't much *but* seed, hundreds per stalk,
a few spare knocked off the cob would do.
Over the state line, first exit sign (you can't
find the camera): "Downer, 1 mile."
At the Flying J near Terre Haute, giants
lumber to the buffet like livestock.
They'll never make it, you think, but then
the bill comes and it's three plates each
piled up with straws and Jell-O and the ends
of fish-sticks. Velvet at the checkout preens
at the mention of her unique handle —
says she's heard of fourteen other Velvets,
but just one with her middle name:
"When the doll came out, I ran right out

and got one." Though she's not real sure
why the name didn't catch: like
Crystal or Chyna or Cheyenne.

This is both geography and biography,
feel free to jump in whenever you want...

Looked at briefly, it seems clear what this is,
where it might have come from.
Like this hammer, for example —
how to pick it up, what to do with it.
Sink a nail, of course, then use the claw
to dry your drawers, cash out a car window.
Just (exactly) like a bird, which stands for nothing
but itself, though it sometimes conjures
a pleasant noise, for some, even reminiscent
of a song, while for the bird, and for today
— the only conversation that means anything
now — it's just noise, a troubling of the air.
In such landscapes, what can you truly know
of anything: of trucking trends or travellers'
diarrhea or the grooming preferences of birds?
You read meaning into tarmac test strips, faces,
during piss breaks scanning the tabloids
filled with personal ads for "rural singles,"
or at roadside oases where you pause, bleary,
for a map or a book-on-tape or a weather warning.
For that matter, what could they really know
(if that's even a word anymore) about us,
about themselves — bright bristling rushing
surfaces, running lights and wind farms
and vanity plates. Arena rock and Golden Miles;

improv demolition derby courses next to
clumsy roadside Calvarys; White Castles and
giant inflatable gorillas colliding in the dark,
following pioneer wagon trails and diverted
creek run-offs, past towering Quonsets,
light-jewelled refinery catwalks, while the
graying muscle of the continent groans, turns
over: constant, rolling, hopeful, unimpressed.

In a Way,

canal is an improvement on *river*
and thought precludes effective action
in a way too complicated to acknowledge
bright birds are airborne messages, in the
way a fountain knows its square, a cactus
is a low-maintenance tenant, the same way
truckers are lumber, cement is a fluid version
of concrete, black is gray and up is down

in a way a street is wide as the word, the
same way my shirt looks better with these stains,
or a window seems bigger when empty,
in the way a fatal blunder brings relief, a list
is a diverting narrative, and clouds are flags
and waves are arrows — a way past malice,
hope or sensation — the way a lobster is a giant,
pugilistic shrimp, a beehive means industry,

an anthill connotes destruction, and Mae
West is synonymous with the Old West.
A raindrop is a harbinger of asphyxia in much
the same way a tear loves a pressure drop,
Stewart Granger is an antonym for Texas Ranger,
a centipede connotes mathematical intrigue,
and one way usually means "no way"—
a way no circle tires of repeating

Counterpane

Hello, lady people! Pigeons are good.
Winter is good. Stoolpigeons are good —
though they're in league with the government,
trying to kill all spontaneity.
Hello everyone! Time to start losing.
Losing is good. Losing is what we came
here to do, and it's going quite well,
thanks for asking.

This morning I was passed by a minivan,
"Someday" printed on the vanity plate.
I wonder what she meant? "Someday soon,
goin' with you" or "I'm gonna get out of
here someday?" or "Someday my prince,
or a real rain's going to come."

Given the words in advance, it
might all be easier. Interpretation —
that's where the problems start.
Take *counterpane*, for an example.
Sounds like a magician's con,
a glass counter you'd bounce coins
off, but really it means something
comforting — a blanket to keep you warm.

Coins bounce off the counterpane
and under that blanket, where they exist
now in the mind only, and so will multiply
at my request. Nothing too greedy,

enough for coffee and a newspaper,
somewhere I can look for a job, anything
to reverse the recent downturn.

People like people who stand for things.
Like Shakespeare arrived at Ellis Island with
a trussed-up suitcase and the equivalent of
$3.50 in badly out-of-date currency.
And look where he ended up.
A real job — I'd like that.
People like people who have jobs.
People like people who stand for things.

Sundial

You drop into conversation like an
afternoon dives into an empty swimming
pool — gamely but down an element.

It's a fall day and a short week,
the streetcar's cavern backlit with heads
and arms: a turkey shoot, a roach motel.

You say you feel qualified to talk
about the service here, having served up
so many slices of yourself over the years.

You've grown weak from bowling olives
at free radicals and chained pit bulls —
their days (both of them) are numbered.

I have my rant about transience and intransigence.
You like to run down the simile as a viable
artistic strategy — you call it "sex through

a sheet," but the way you call it that
makes it so vividly sexy: the sheet
with my name on it, the sad euphemism

lugeing its way toward the gap,
downspout, spinning into unknown.
I was told this was how they vote in Japan,

but I'm not sure I believe a word of it
anymore: that raft of rabble and nogoodniks,
their avowed allegiance to the way things stand.

And so we scroll through the hours, like the
fireball scours the skin of a bank tower:
tireless rehearsal of the dark scenes in tow.

Plenty

The sky, lit up like a question or
an applause meter, is beautiful
like everything else today: the leaves
in the gutters, salt stains on shoes,
the girl at the IGA who looks just like
Julie Delpy, but you don't tell her —
she's too young to get the reference and
coming from you it'll just seem creepy.
So much beauty today you can't find
room for it, closets already filled
with beautiful trees and smells and
glances and clever turns of phrase.
Behind the sky there's a storm
on the way, which, with your luck,
will be a beautiful storm — dark
clouds beautiful as they arguably are,
the rain beautiful as it always is —
even lightning can be beautiful in a
scary kind of way (there's a word
for that, but let's forget it for the moment).
And maybe the sun will hang in long
enough to light up a few raindrops —
like jewels or glass or those bright beads
girls put between the letters on the
bracelets that spell out their beautiful names —
Skye or Miranda or Verandah — which isn't
even a name, although it is a word
we use to call things what they are,
and would be a pleasant place to sit

and watch the beautiful sky, beautiful
storm, the people with their beautiful
names walking toward the lake
in lovely clothing saying unpleasant
things over the phone about the people
they work with, all of it just adding to the
mother lode, the *surfeit* of beauty,
which on this day is just a fancy way
of saying lots, too much, skidloads, plenty.

JERAMY DODDS

Crabwise to the Hounds

"We are only allowed to live / due to some colossal mis-understanding," writes Jeramy Dodds in this astonishing first book. The exploration of this misunderstanding is the subject of *Crabwise to the Hounds*, and Dodds' language confronts the entropy with some wondrous chaos of its own. There is a cyclonic lexical energy here, deep intelligence, and a serious commitment to craft. His poems build and infold all at once, and opposing forces create incredible tension in them: the reader's mouth, open in awe, next barks a disbelieving laugh. There's more than a little of Buster Keaton here, threading his body through a window in a falling wall. The author seems *sui generis* at first, but then you sense how lightly he's stepped through the bramble of various inheritances to find his own voice, and on the first try. In "Making Sure," for instance, Dodds harnesses both Tim Lilburn and William Stafford at the same moment as he's claiming a certain territory for his own now: the natural world occupied by an ineluctable machinery. He builds against it this machine of language in which Glenn Gould negotiates the Danube, Ho Chi Minh has gone to "repair / the night through a colander of stars," the aviary has a recovery wing, and even the act of sipping water is reinvented. A research archaeologist by training, Dodds is sounding the deeps here. A marvellous debut.

Lions of the Work Week

It was the year I subscribed to an absurd
number of magazines. There were lions everywhere.
Lions at the tambourines, lions in the gatehouse, lions
up the sleeve of your bible-black dress, you could set your watch
by the screams, the shimmy-shackle of claws
on the hardwood floor wore down your ear, ghosts
of lions fathered our kids, lions of the long grass,
Barnum & Bailey types, we knelt at the scimitar scar
on the tamer's breast as valets brought lions upon lions,
lions going at us with the violence of a clearance sale, my wife
comes home with a lion between her legs, antelope musk
hog-tied in her mouth, bed-lamp–bright wounds,
a yoke of tear-jars tingling from her nicked shoulders,
lions cornered in her cranium, the wedding dancers slain,
their scattered organs like gobs of fruit, lions
at the chink in our *amour*, lions on the owls, lions
like Labs, the house pets snapped, lions loaded for bear,
lions at the crypt ledger jotting down kills,
plaster casts of claws above our cancer-ward doors, lions
parted the curtains of our ribs, panted like whistling arrows,
starved lions, hair painted on their bones,
lions in the yard with the kids, lions
at the midnight fridge, chicken on their lips,
lions at the watering hole bullying
for beer money, lions mowing through
the Foot Guard, Beefeaters, Dragoons,
standing in perfect pecking order
at my bedside, waiting for me to snap
the bones of my watch to my wrist
and dress in their gift of slipper-thin armour.

Prosthetics

> *Despite all the amputations you know you could just go out*
> *and dance to the rock and roll stations, and it was all right.*
> — *Lou Reed*

I'm on the pier with my back against
the wrecking machine. Cyclones of terns
turn atop prop-churned debris.
This morning I feel like the wheel
you fell asleep at. Godstruck by the flag
clotted on its pole like the skin of a starved
animal. The downcoast ferry's
run out of hearing. A spaghetti-strap dress,
a trembling gin, as you shift weight
to your wooden leg.

Ear to a conch, I hear
acrobats in waiting rooms
flipping through magazines,
the gull squawk of the guitarist's hand
going to chord, stunt men falling
through awning after awning.
The sea is a soliloquy
in a buried warehouse.

But March is the month of swollen doors.
Boots bark through checkerweaves of ice.
Lacking prophylactics, we pull apart
to watch our dead sons run along your one
good leg. Hitting the deck, they hoist dust
to their meniscus shoulders.

The sea, a surface unworn by our movement.
Our shore leave, a landscape painted
with a brush made
from the hair of the dog
of those storm-closed roads,
as though a gale had come to town
and left wearing pelicans.

Making Sure

Deer, a jackrabbit the size of a motorcycle.
  — Tim Lilburn

Hit quick, the road-wasted stag
fell like the sick sorrel horse
we hunted by syringe
in a 3 x 5 pen. His fallen
figure-skater sprawl
drew out our awe, lying
on his own canvas of blood,
iron tailings from a ran-down mill.
Overcoated men with leather bags
of tinctures and bitters
couldn't bring him around.
Witnesses stood, arms crossed,
afraid their hands might reach
for the debris of muscle guyropes
knifed by the blunt bumper of an SUV.
Looking aside I saw
a young woman come out
of the woods and work
her way through the crowd,
coming to rest in a kneel
at the buck's breast.
We moved to halt her
but she heeled us with one hand
while the other slid to his snapped
sapling crown. She rubbed her fingers
gently down his brow, grappling his snout
to bring his half-yard of neck right round.

Second Glance at Corrag

Out of the morass he looked like
a reconstructed grenade. Pelt burdened
by burrs. Corroded cloak pin of his cant-hook claws.
The bulrushes gave their windhead nods.
At his lope, spores backstep and scatter.
And that spine scar where the key enters and winds.
The beehive of his eyes sends droids to probe
the switchgrass. So still, the windsocks
hung like daggered lungs. His bible is a flipbook
of practical anatomy. His sightline, a river
you can't talk across. An inmate running his tin cup
along the bars is the muscle-headed bruise racing
inside his ribs like a motorbike in a cage ball.
From southern cape to southern cape
his lungs are a harrow's width apart.
His cochlea is a spoon-dug tunnel beneath
the pet cemetery, his saphenous nerve, a boy
with a bouquet of fresh horses. His irises are owls
and owls are cached hunks of bonfire soot.
His hunger strike does not include giving up fellatio.
Veins are a Gorgon's black-adder bouffant.
Capillaries are winter maples scrubbing the mist.
Blood cells are dust-taxied down a flashlight's path.
His mouth is my mother crying in the car wash.
Dew-worm hunters hatch kerosene lamps
on the gospel choir of his brain
while he comes crawling in his Sunday best,
as though his spine were a bell rope
at midnight and the village vacant
and his father had gone to town
with his inheritance — an Alsatian
that was a dowry for the distance
he'd cross day after dawn after dusk.

The Official Translation of Ho Chi Minh's
August 18th, 1966, Telephone Call

Tell me the windows aren't really sweating.

You should come back when I've something better to wear.

I'm sorry but no one could tell me the time
and I was worried I'd be late.

The birds are the ones pulling out the rain.

After it's all down, it makes the outdoors like a basement.

I can see the antennae are bored.

I'm tall, but not as tall as my shadow would allow.

There are no church bells, but gates
often rattle on their latches.

My favourite line in a newspaper story:
He brought up the gun and let it go.

My favourite sign:
Those likely to die on the premises are strongly discouraged.

My favourite thing about America
is the inhale sound of cars on the streets after rain.

The last time I heard her name it was breaking through my sleep.

In the sky are hills of weather.

The croissant really isn't that great.

I hear shouts and stay away from the curfewed parts of town.

I swear the garbage truck arrives earlier each week.

Before you came, I saw clouds waterfalling over the mountains.

When I'm out for dinner I never want to meet the cook;
I just don't want to know.

The front step of my aunt's house dips at its centre.

When you came, the wind drew back in.

I have seen him wandering through camp talking to his feet
as if they were a dog.

I worry about people washing their cars late at night.

I'm more worried about the way you drive
than the number of drinks you've had.

The bat-winged junks are lovingly filled with RPGs.

Things I will never hold:
the lightning on the sun, the diamonds of the sea...

*[On the tape he leaves the telephone and you can hear the sound of
latches tumbling, sheets flapping on the line, a match striking. He
coughs in the distance before returning to add:]*

If, by the time you get here, the telephone

is dangling from its carriage

and emptying into the room, it is

because I have gone outside to repair

the night through a colander of stars.

Crown Land

North of lumberless land,
we made the animals fight for us.
Sore warped beasts pinched off
the rag-and-bone rack, ones that
bit by barbed bit were forced to
fisticuffs in the scrub slump of hills.
With a hairline rapture these animals
came and went about our days,
leaving their young to defend
the palaces they were forced from
for us. These carousel mammals walked
skewered to the pole. With forepaws
in kid gloves they pricked ears when
tinder sticks lapped the brass-green
kettledrums, drums that laid down the miles
to their relevant demise.

After rock-picking, the fields
were pocked. My uncle with a hazel switch
kicking his mule's hide. My uncle
after twenty more one-mores, his
hat-hidden forehead facing hindsight
as he ox-eyed the ten-ton dewline
that girdled the drumlins. His
cat-o'-nine-tailed spine
humped along the timber-slab paths,
his blinkered mule craning at the headlands;
his pelt hides bone anchor points, marrow levers,
sanguine pulleys. An oilcloth dropped
on his doily-thin, God-given name.

And that's our house, dog-eared
by a balepick hooked in the gatepost
like a tongue licked on winter tin. From
a Caesarean cloudbelly, grey hounds of rain
tear messenger pigeons down to half-tilled fallow.
From the crown of the fox tower I pull my scope
from its rat-hide case, come in close on Uncle,
that mule under his loins scraping home
in ankle drags. The gully was as far as I got
by eye. The rest I only heard,
the noise I'm writing to forget
as the barren hounds got onto him.

A. F. MORITZ

The Sentinel

A. F. Moritz has beautiful command of what William
Empson called "a long delicate rhythm based on straight
singing lines." In his extraordinary collection *The Sentinel*,
we never lose our bearing, so sure is his formal grace,
even as we are carried into fabulous circumstance, get
lost in places we know, are found in imaginary cities or
in any "prosperous country." We read his fable of a city
awaiting the arrival of a butterfly and stand with the
crowd in wonder, as a creature so large it blots out the
sun transforms to "a humble yellow thing," so menacing
and loud it crashes to the sea "like a fighter jet" but erupts
in "a burst of quiet." After such a dazzling show, we are
left with unreadable feelings to watch "the black ocean
again." It is a place Moritz often asks us to stand. He
is at once moved and troubled by "the black imperial /
Roman traces" that our language shares with the classi-
cal poets, numbering himself among the barbarians
with their "slaughter / and triumph." In the title poem, the
one keeping watch — a figure, we now know, for the poet —
stands on either side of two forms of darkness, "the
outward / dark before his face" and the dark of the camp
at his back, where he imagines soldiers settling down
to sleep. Their "dreams / of bleeding inwardly" are the
dreams of this unsettling, superb collection of poems.

What We Had

I really did love you in a sense, colleagues,
friends and fellow citizens and passersby
of my day here, who stormed the smoking world,
struggling to plant your flags or at least be heard.
I looked at you with consistent and unfeigned
interest, delighted in the revelation
of your pointless variety. It was joy to know
myself a poet among so many who knew
it also, but kept it quiet — the one thing
you did keep quiet. So many males and females
of divers pretensions: fortified handmade heights
from which in rage and fear you each would look
downward at me and melt in love. And I
would melt too and would feel the sympathy
of living with you among the flowers and rocks,
and dream sometimes for long seconds on end
that all any of you wanted was blessèd life
for everyone, and me too. But she and I
clung to each other, comrades, and I understood
that you more truly were the storm, and though
the two of us are dead now, what we had
to do in life, in fact, was to survive you.

Old Pet

Come, my body, leap up, while you still can,
onto my knees, into my lap. Come let me pet you,
comfort you and take comfort while there's time,
while you last. How calm you are: content, it seems,
with your infirmity, your age, in the almost changeless
youth of your soft hide, your pelt and shy quiet,
expressionless as you huddle and crouch for this leap
you can still make, though it's grown great, this petty
piece of your young and many springs.

Why did I never, body, cherish you enough?
Although I thought I was spending all my minted hours
on you, till I'd cry at the long waste of time, chained
by eyes and tongue, the ends of every extremity,
to your pleasure. Now I can't recall ever once
kissing you, lying locked in you, deep as I want.

You'll die, it won't be long, body, swiftly
in animal nobility — how you wear your decline unnoticing,
the way a poor man walks in his only shirt to work —
and then, without you, in what mud of my own
making will I linger, falling apart? Purr now
and fuse your old pleasure into crotch of my torso,
palm of my hand, vision of eyes and sag of diaphragm
inseparably: they're yours. Give me your indifference
that a once forest-wide range comes down
to couch and counter now, and this lap. Give me
your unrepentant having-known
a more-than-ant's-intimacy with the grass,

a more-than-god's-innocence in the hunt,
a greater-than-winged-agility in branches
and light. Leap up, body, while you still can,
let me finally hold you, feel you, close enough.

The Jar

We found a jar there. Not a vase, not a piece of the potter's art
but glass, from a store shelf, with a threaded mouth,
the lid and label long gone, all residue of the product blotted away:
bright crystal. I had to tell you this because the word jar
dwells in between comprehending both. It reminded us of songs we know,
the "broken water jar," the "jar in Tennessee," the "drinkin' liquor
from an old fruit jar." But the desolating place: white weeds,
white ground baked into sharp lumps and ridges,
a dead sapling, bushes crisp with thirst, rattling in a breeze.
No moisture in the jar. No way to tell if it had been thrown away
or washed and kept as a vessel. We succeeded for a while in seeing
the curves and sun-glints of its strange perfect hollow with affection.
We felt shaken, imprisoned, as though the low whine of the acres of flies,
as though the silence, were aftermath of a deafening shout. We longed
for wet darkness, even if it brought that doom-laden bird, the nightjar.

The Tidal Wave

One day I'll wake and see the tidal wave above my city
fulgurating at its dripping diamond crest in the sun
like another, a nearer, sun, and its sheer wall
under its beautiful crown of spume will be
a vertical plain wider than any on earth, a bare steppe
but of flesh, flesh of planed and planished liquid
teak and jet and jade.
How tall will it be — three miles, a hundred miles? How far
or imminent? Will there be seconds or years
before it falls on us? I only know it won't matter anymore
that I was sick in mind. Under the shadow or in the light
of the wave I remembered childhood,
when I dewinged a moth, inspected
the writhing tube and then forgot, went elsewhere.
And manhood, when the memory came back one day
twenty years later and so I couldn't reach the moth
to give the gift of murder, impose release
on its horror as the pure ignorance
of my imagination created it
and felt it. This I thought of every day and hour
to the exclusion of battling like everyone
with everyone for the bread reserved
to others. I slipped into alley mouths
and doorways among empty buildings and occupied
myself all day with saying my nightly prayers, O God
please take away the carcinoma, aphasia, ataxia,
the monomania, hysteria, dementia from her
and him, the age from them, aren't they old
enough already, why should they have to get

still older, till the list of them
became so long that many died
as I forgot them, as my day
became not long enough to run through the vast roll
and pronounce it all. I lost
who they were in the bourdon of their names
rumbling in me, shaking the frame
till I thought my ears were bleeding and I clawed
my skull — but nothing was happening there, in fact I,
the face that faced it, looked roseate, glimpsed
in dark windows, and cheerful. A conscious eminence
absorbed in guilt and supplication, scraggy psalms,
while the citizens ran on and soon forgot
the ones at the gate fallen
with broken leg and twisted bowels and waiting and hoping
to be shot. But when the wave appears
above the city, all this will proceed as usual,
it's what we know, and the absolute equality
of what I do and what they do, my strength and theirs,
will appear in the water's black and crystal glow.

The Sentinel

The one who watches while the others sleep
does not see. It is hoped, it is to be hoped
there is nothing to see. The camp has quieted
behind him and all is peace there — let it be —
at his back, where he longs to turn his face
and see the walls of pitched cloth that hide
his comrades, sleeping. But lights go down, and out,
and if he turned there would be nothing, black,
with just the bulks of looming tents aglow
with just the memory of last evening's light.
Likewise, nothing to see in the outward
dark before his face, where there is nothing,
it is to be hoped — only a darkness
of useless vigilance, unless it is a darkness
of hostile conniving lights not lit out there,
surrounding treachery, faces smeared with ash
to blend in with the night and lying low.
And what if morning ever comes, when things
are just as always, it's obvious to all?
Won't he have to find some commander and report
everything he observed? Out and beyond
the perimeter, he notes nothing that may not be
a moth fluttering or a shooting star
behind thick cloud. Within the camp, though,
constant stirrings. Sudden snorts as if breath
cut off by some torturer was suddenly permitted,
the hands unclenched from the throat at the last
second before death. And longer, steady snores,
woodmen in snowy forests. Whimpers of mothers'

and pet dogs' names, uncertain breezes moist
with tears and snot fluttering the tent flaps,
men curled up knees to nose and heels to hips
like ringed camps and feeling only
the anus's openness and the back a target,
or stretched out straight, cupping and tangling fingers
in hair and cooing to the genitals as if
to a girlfriend. Fart, belch, and vomit,
urine, dirt and sperm falling in latrines,
shuffle of feet on stones, books, letters, pictures
felt for under brittle pillows and the dreams
of bleeding inwardly, of growing a third arm,
of removing the penis like a banana from its skin
and passing it around the campfire, vaguely anxious
the others won't pass it back. But
the commanders, wouldn't they tell him:
What good's this report? You saw nothing
you were supposed to see. You wasted your time
listening to us, but we knew where we were
and what was going on here. And you saw only
the obvious and trivial and drew the worst conclusions.
Or drew no conclusions, it's simply that the obvious
always looks filthy: any obstruction you can't pass
or at least see through takes the form to you
of a rotting cellar wall aswarm with worms.
Besides, none of this ever happened. You
made it up to humiliate us, you are a foreign
agent, which is why no hint of the enemy's
numbers, movements, or power ever appears
anywhere in your lying reports. You fell asleep
at your sacred post and this report records
your evil dreams, a spontaneous creation you love

and so a deeper shame to you than if
you had rationally constructed out of sheer depravity
this libel on your comrades. And who
appointed you at all? You are not the sentinel.
The sentinel has already given his intelligence,
which we are analyzing. You are the lonely watcher,
the one who won't sleep until it's time to work,
the one who wants a salary and a title
for insomnia. If we have nightmares,
it's that we hear your footsteps under our window,
wake up, look out along the street: no one.
That's what they'll say. And yet the report
will have to be filed, the storm endured. But not till dawn.
It is almost possible, it would almost be possible
to enjoy this fogged-in darkness, this dewfall and
rustling silence, the accustomed expectation
of receiving the first shot if indeed the enemy
has chosen tonight, except that one can't relax,
each detail must be noted or the report
will be a lie. In fact through no fault of his own
the sentinel will miss something, and the report
he contemplates, or the refusal to report
he also contemplates, will be a traitorous lie.
To light a match might well draw fire. He strikes,
it doesn't catch. But no, it sputters, waits,
then flares. He moves it to his lips, and peace.

Dandelion

Through the infinite limits of the night in ruins
the mumbler goes with his sounds but they're all one:
voices cut in pieces, pain that oozes
from the dead scars along this flat terrain
that channel dust past gardens and cottages.
Women come out and sniff him suspiciously:
the same old obsessive hatred of their sex,
flattering but lethal. And me too: I smell
his loneliness. How right to shake my head
and break the spell. I'm wondering again
why dandelions burn so terribly yet cool
on the ragged slope with its wild apple tree.
I'm five years old, absorbed, and soon will hate
the march each dawn I see to the plant gate.
But now to be back is right, my wife with me,
at naked five years old, the trackless field,
the dandelion fire and the wild apple shade.

ABOUT THE POETS

KEVIN CONNOLLY is a poet, journalist, and editor. He has published four collections of poetry, including *drift* (House of Anansi Press, 2005), which won the Trillium Poetry Award. He lives on a cat farm in Toronto's east end with his partner, writer Gil Adamson.

JERAMY DODDS lives in Orono, Ontario. His poems have been translated into Finnish, French, Latvian, Swedish, German and Icelandic. In 2007 he held a residency at the Baltic Centre for Writers and Translators on the island of Gotland, Sweden. He is the winner of the 2006 Bronwen Wallace Memorial Award and the 2007 CBC Literary Award in poetry. He works as a research archaeologist and co-edits for littlefishcartpress.

MICK IMLAH was born in 1956 and brought up near Glasgow and in Kent. He was editor of *Poetry Review* from 1983 to 1986, and worked at the *Times Literary Supplement* since 1992. He edited *The New Penguin Book of Scottish Verse* (with Robert Crawford, 2000) and made selections of the poems of Tennyson and Edwin Muir for Faber and Faber. *The Lost Leader* is Mick Imlah's first collection of poetry in twenty years. The book won the 2008 Forward Prize and was shortlisted for the 2008 T.S. Eliot Prize. In the autumn of 2007 Mick Imlah was diagnosed with motor neurone disease (also known as ALS/Lou Gehrig's disease) and he died on January 12, 2009. He is survived by his partner, Maren Meinhardt, and their two daughters.

DEREK MAHON was born in Belfast in 1941, and studied French literature at Trinity College Dublin and at the Sorbonne. He lived for many years in London, England, working variously as a reviewer, adaptor of literary texts for British television, and poetry editor of the *New Statesman*. More recently he has lived in Dublin and Kinsale. He is regarded as one of the most accomplished and influential of contemporary Irish poets. He has influenced not only a younger generation of British and Irish poets but has also been one of the influences on a new school of Scandinavian poets centred in Oslo and Gothenburg. He has been described as one of the most musical of poets now writing in English. Derek Mahon received the 2007 David Cohen Prize, for recognition of a lifetime's achievement in literature.

A. F. MORITZ has written fifteen books of poetry, and has received the Guggenheim Fellowship, the Award in Literature of the American Academy and Institute of Arts and Letters, and the Ingram Merrill Fellowship, and has been a finalist for the Governor General's Literary Award. His collection *Night Street Repairs* (House of Anansi Press, 2004) won the ReLit Award, and he was awarded *Poetry* magazine's Bess Hokin Prize for his poem, "The Sentinel." Moritz lives in Toronto and teaches at Victoria College, University of Toronto.

C. D. WRIGHT was born and raised in the Ozark Mountains of Arkansas. She has published twelve previous poetry collections. Her collaboration with photographer Deborah Luster, a journey into the prison-industrial complex entitled *One Big Self*, was honoured with a Lange-Taylor Prize from the Center for Documentary Studies. Wright has also received fellowships from the MacArthur Foundation, the Guggenheim Foundation, the National Endowment for the Arts, and the Lannan Foundation. In the 1990s she served for five years as the State Poet of Rhode Island. Wright is currently the Israel J. Kapstein Professor of English at Brown University, and lives outside Providence, Rhode Island.

DEAN YOUNG has published eight previous books, most recently *elegy on toy piano,* which was named a finalist for the Pulitzer Prize, and *Embryoyo.* His collection *Skid* was a finalist for the Lenore Marshall Prize. Young has received fellowships from the Guggenheim Foundation and the National Endowment for the Arts. In 2007 he received an Academy Award in Literature from the American Academy of Arts and Letters. He teaches at The Writers' Workshop at the University of Iowa and in the Warren Wilson Low Residency Program. Dean Young divides his time between Berkeley, California, and Iowa City, Iowa, residing with his wife, the novelist Cornelia Nixon.

ACKNOWLEDGEMENTS

The publisher thanks the following for their kind permission to reprint the work contained in this volume:

"Lions of the Work Week," "Prosthetics," "Making Sure," "Second Glance at Corrag," "The Official Translation of Ho Chi Minh's August 18th, 1966, Telephone Call," and "Crown Land" from *Crabwise to the Hounds* by Jeramy Dodds are reprinted by permission of Coach House Books.

"Muck," "The Ayrshire Orpheus," "Drink v. Drugs," and "Iona," from *The Lost Leader* by Mick Imlah are reprinted by permission of Faber and Faber.

"Insomnia," "The Lady from the Sea," "Art Notes" Parts 1, 2, and 4, "Homage to Gaia" Parts 1 and 5, and "Homage to Goa" from *Life on Earth* by Derek Mahon are reprinted by permission of The Gallery Press.

The excerpt from "Rising, Falling, Hovering" from *Rising, Falling, Hovering* by C.D. Wright is reprinted by permission of Copper Canyon Press.

"Self Search," "Gruss," "Briar," "Fire Ode," "Lives of the Primitives," and "Exit Exam," from *Primitive Mentor* by Dean Young are reprinted by permission of University of Pittsburgh Press.